OLD MAN HOWLING
AT THE MOON

PROSE POEMS

Peter Johnson

MADHAT PRESS
ASHEVILLE, NORTH CAROLINA

MadHat Press
MadHat Incorporated
PO Box 8364, Asheville, NC 28814

The Library of Congress has assigned
this edition a Control Number of
2018952130

ISBN 978-1-941196-76-2 (paperback)

Cover art by Marc Vincenz
Cover design by Marc Vincenz
Book design by MadHat Press

www.MadHat-Press.com

First Printing

For my old-guy friends: Richard Elkington, Kevin Johnson, James Myers, Richard Murphy, Rod Philbrick, Walker Rumble, and the four Toms: Bogucki, Cesarz, O'Donnell, and Schaner.

OTHER BOOKS BY PETER JOHNSON

Prose Poetry

Pretty Happy!
Miracles & Mortifications
Eduardo & "I"
Rants and Raves: Selected and New Prose Poems
Love Poems for the Millennium (a chapbook)

Young Adult/Adult

What Happened
Loserville
Out of Eden: A Thriller
I'm a Man: Short Stories

Middle Grade

The Amazing Adventures of John Smith Jr., AKA Houdini
The Life and Times of Benny Alvarez
The Night Before Krampus

TABLE OF CONTENTS

Part I

Part II

Coda

There are moments in life when true invective is called for,
when there comes an absolute necessity, out of a deep sense
of justice, to denounce, mock, vituperate, lash out, rail at,
in the strongest possible language.

‛ —CHARLES SIMIC

The poet is there
So that the tree does not grow crooked.

—NICANOR PARRA

Each creature on earth has a headache the size of its own head.

—E. C. OSONDU

PREFACE

"In Praise of Anger, Along with a Very Brief History of the Complaint"

There's not a lot of anger in contemporary America poetry, which is surprising because there's so much to be angry about. But there *is* an inordinate amount of fashionable irony. Fashionable irony doesn't get under anyone's skin, and with all the grants and awards out there, it makes sense not to piss off anyone.

Still, I've always been a fan of angry poets. I've always felt a kinship with whiners like Catullus, Nicanor Parra—even Charles Bukowski when he wrote his best stuff. Ginsberg's "America" is also high on my list. These poets had a way of merging outrage and humor, the ability to attack people and institutions without acting superior. Their personae were often so self-conscious, so prone to self-loathing, that it was hard not to view them somewhat ironically. Although much of the work associated with the above poets, and many others I could name, might be called invectives or satires, or in Parra's case, "antipoetry," I would prefer to name them "complaints." There is a long history of complaint literature. It's a genre that reached its height in 14th-century France and, as one critic points out, has generally been "voiced in many forms, such as the protest poem, political song, satire, and sermon, as well as other modes such as narrative, lyric, ballad, drama, treatise, letters, and even romance." Coincidentally, then, complaint literature, like the prose poem itself, has a history of borrowing from and subverting many different genres.

One reason I prefer the term "complaint" for the prose poems in *Old Man Howling at the Moon* is because the term embraces both older and contemporary notions of the word. The Grumpy Old Everyman in these poems is frustrated and angry, and he wants you to know it. He's a ranter and a raver. He's outraged and outrageous. But he can also be funny in a black-humorish kind of way. As Parra said, "Humor makes contact with the reader easier. Remember, it's when you lose your sense of humor that you begin to reach for your pistol."

I think my Grumpy Old Everyman would agree with Parra's take on humor, though he would probably still keep his pistol cocked, loaded, and concealed under his pillow at night, just in case he needed it.

Considering these troubled times, how can we blame him?

PART I

Houdini Weenie

For this trick, a time machine, a little ore dust, and a smokestack staining the sky with chemicals.

Add a fat boy, locked in his room while a party's rip-and-roar rattles holy statues on his dresser.

It's me, gentle reader, sent to bed for shattering McMahon's picture window, for eating the coconut icing before the first "Happy Birthday" broke wind, for calling Aunt Esther an alien and having the goods to prove it.

Through a crack in the door, I see her husband in cherry-red flip-flops.

He's polishing his glasses with a tissue, smiling at this here unfortunate peeper.

Earlier that day I had read a book on Galileo.

I was hooked on telescopes, searching for the magic ring concealed in cereal boxes of skinny boys, of boys with money and pedigreed dogs.

It's the late 1950s, and through a screened bedroom window, I see a full moon shot full of holes.

And through a screened bedroom window, I tumble, caught an hour later stealing candy from a local drugstore.

"A regular escape artist," my uncle says, shaking his finger at me.

"A regular little Houdini Weenie."

Neil

On the corner, two guys arguing over a can a beer.

I want to break open a box of cartridges but don't own a gun.

I want to complain to my dead friend Neil, who would say, "Smile, it's a good day to be Peter."

I think of Neil as I awake to the Latino's La Cucaracha horn at 6 a.m.

Or shake off my penis for the fifth time in the middle of the night.

Or stand in the rain as if stoned while the dog takes a crap.

This is a life he may have glimpsed before being head-onned by an ice-covered pine tree.

I can still see his wife stumbling down the carpeted aisle, flanked by two Labrador retrievers, a life-size picture of Neil on the altar.

Later, the dogs howling outside like two bruised saxophones while the cheese dip got passed around.

I knew very few people in that church.

How could that be?

So here I am, a little hungover, listening to two guys argue over a can of beer.

Across the hall, my teenage son stirs safely in his bed, oblivious to the many ways people can die.

"It's a good day to be Lucas," Neil would've told him.

"It's a good day to tell your father you love him."

American Male, Acting Up

They say your whole life flashes before you when you die, but I'm sure I'll witness the lives of others.

And if I'm right, please spare me the lives of this moron wearing a black wifebeater, mid-calf jeans, and orange work boots.

We're at the zoo, more precisely the habitat of the arctic fox, whom we've never seen awake, terminally depressed to find himself in a moderately-sized, ethnically-mixed city surrounded by creatures who hurl animal crackers, caw like crows, or scream, "Wake up, stupid."

Which is what this man's two boys are yelling.

When I tell my son to ignore them, he asks, "Why?" and I say, "Because anyone with half a brain wouldn't scare a little fox."

The man glares at me, and I glimpse the chaos of his past lives.

It's the feast of Saturnalia.

He smells of grapes and cheese, the blood of his favorite Thracian slave hardened on his left thigh.

He's swigging diluted wine, exchanging arm punches with friends.

He's the hirsute sweat bag movies portray with thumb downturned.

The one who two thousand years later chugs four beers, then goes to the zoo to torment the animals.

Laugh if you must, but I would gladly take this bully down.

So when he stares, I stare back, and when he says, "Boys, we paid our money, so scream whatever you want," I brace myself, prepare to take a beating.

Cheerleader

There it was: the cheerleader outfit my wife wore when she was seventeen, and how saddened not to be the first to take it off.

Behind a bush, in the back seat of a car, on a beach chair next to Joe Blow's swimming pool.

I wanted to punish her with questions.

Force her to read my friend's penny-dreadful novel.

I imagined her by a water fountain, posing for some halfwit hockey player.

"What could be simpler than to Think Pink," she would say, Old Halfwit stunned still, rooted to the cheap linoleum floor.

I imagined the middle-aged math teacher's front-row grin as she performed her famous midair split.

Our living-room rug was small consolation, worn in spots from hands and knees.

Not even my little book of love poems eased the pain.

"And by the way," I say to her many years later, "of course they respect you for your mind, so ignore their groans when you bend over to retrieve a pencil, or reach for a file on top of your desk."

And Nothing Else Matters

On I-395 between Occum and Preston the interstate ablaze with foliage, a heavy metal ballad swelling the speakers of my SUV, I weep like the old fool I am.

My wife called me from Providence to say Sue Anne overdosed in a motel in North Carolina when she was supposed to be alive in a motel in White Plains.

Supposedly because of a man, which is another way of saying *Fate*.

Supposedly because of her mother, which is another way of saying *Love*.

Whoever is sick will become well. Whoever is well will become sick.

If I credit this passage to Aquinas, will it console you?

Will you drive to North Carolina and empty Sue Anne's belongings into a cardboard box?

Will you collapse at the next rest stop, very much like this one, where a family of pine trees, very much like these, bends from the weight of the wind, paying homage to a god much kinder than ours?

Special

They say everyone deserves someone special, but I know people who don't.

Like the ones who didn't visit when I sat lame on my frigid front porch, reading Faulkner and sipping lycopene-laced green tea.

But squirrels came with their empty stomachs, and telemarketers phoned in their hollow promises.

Cars passed, too, with their steely glares.

And that was something.

I was shaking my cane at a stay-at-home mom from across the street.

She was leaning on a baby jogger, taunting me.

"You're lazy," she yelled. "You're giving me the creeps."

I smiled, hoping a blood vessel might burst inside her head.

"I ain't quittin' yet," I yelled, leveling my cane at her.

At the time, I was trying to write something important.

A hopeful book a stay-at-home mom might read.

A book a truck driver wouldn't throw out the window to make room for a fifteen-year-old runaway, who'd go down on him in Reno for a ride to L.A.

Hurricane

They were watching a hurricane on TV, hoping someone would die.

But just a weatherman with a receding hairline blown onto his ass.

They were hoping someone would take a chance.

Suck on a downed power line or leap insanely off a pier wearing a circa-17th-century life preserver.

Which is to say wearing nothing at all.

In this poem the "they" is "you":

The uniformed hotel doorman, the short-order cook, the seamstress, the bulldozer operator making a terrible scene at the dentist's.

Yes, it's you, whose better self gave up years ago, succumbing to stupidity and boredom.

Hurricanes, tsunamis, massacres, droughts.

This is how you live, waiting for death to nudge you with its big black horn.

"Hurricane"—from the Spanish *huracán,* from Taino *hurákan;* akin to Arawak *kulakani,* "thunder."

Can you hear it?

Heraclitus

I was fifteen and studying ancient Greek when the Jesuits took us to see a movie about Heraclitus.

It was a hundred times longer than his fragments.

Everyone knows the one about not stepping into the same river twice, but few are aware of his lost treatise on the nose.

Man, do I have a whopper sinus infection today.

I'm in bed watching a cardinal limping on a limb.

He's agitated, screeching like a castrato who just realized the profundity of his loss.

Imagine that kind of despair.

Still,

Sick or castrated, how can you not marvel at spring?

Those days when it's enough to wander mindlessly through a vineyard or to tiptoe like a tuba through a particularly difficult melody.

Heraclitus wrote a lot about wisdom and fire but very little about anything that blooms.

You certainly wouldn't call his prose "muscular."

All up in his head, like most of his fellow ass-scratchers whose endless and, excuse me, pointless analytical leaps leave very little room for a soft landing.

Which has always been my preference.

I'll opt for the safe oversize slogan any day.

Give me the sixth hole at Firefly on a windy November day, too cold for anything metaphorical to happen.

11

Love Story

We broke down in a little seaside town where soap made from whale sperm went for ten dollars a bar.

The car mechanic bragged his TV had only three channels, and that everyone's house smelled like meatloaf.

While he fixed the car, we lunched on the beach, desperately needing to create a "moment" to remember when our yet-to-be-born children would hate us.

I stroked her hair, told her the human brain was like a shower nozzle.

She compared it to a skunk, but neither of us could explain the grounds of likeness.

It was the Death-of-Metaphor Decade.

You could say a car looked like a tropical fish and no one got it.

Walking the beach, we discovered a worn leather glove and debated its history.

Then we took a chilling tour of a local winery.

When we paid the mechanic, he said that if every living chicken were lined up, they'd circle the earth eight times.

A sad and troubling fact, but it was time to leave, the town disappearing behind us as if it had never existed.

My Father Wasn't an Alcoholic

He didn't wet his pants at my First Communion or make drunken passes at my girlfriends.

He didn't beat my mother or hide his bottle of Scotch in the baby's room.

He never stumbled or puked in public.

For years, he rode a crane and delivered the mail.

He never dropped a load of steel on anyone or stole welfare checks.

He didn't teach me how to swing a bat, or slobber obscenities when I struck out.

He wasn't even at the game.

He was riding a crane, for Christ's sake; he was delivering the mail.

I was my own masthead, my own backfield in motion.

Can't blame him if my antlers got battered.

He never rolled me a fat one or brought Jack Daniel's to my lips.

Never cut my face out of the family photo album.

He wasn't an alcoholic.

He wasn't a mean man.

In fact, he was rarely even home.

Talkin' 'Bout My Generation

"The end of a poem should sound like the click when a box closes."

Whose box?

Not mine.

I don't even own a box that clicks.

Just one of the many lies we've been told, or tell each other—about this current war, for instance.

Or that we'll live to be eighty without drooling all over ourselves.

What fools and liars—all of us at Woodstock, stoned on drugs and sex, when in fact we were home cutting the front lawn or enrolled in Kaplan courses.

All of us protesting the war when in fact we were stretched out on couches, hungover, watching reruns of *I Love Lucy* while well-paid doctors swore we had twelve toes and four testicles.

And free love?

Invented by men, for men.

Even my father knew that.

We're the ones who won't say boo! to our children, who listen to rock and roll sell SUVs, golf balls, tampons.

And let's not forget my friend who dropped acid with his son, crooning "Yellow Submarine" into a camcorder.

Something meaningful to share while he's dying of prostate cancer, saving up cash to freeze himself for the next century.

How's that for The Big Chill?
How's that for t-t-t-t-talkin' 'bout my generation…?

The Robert Bly Affair

for R. E.

It happened the year I began calling myself Tomaz and having lengthy public conversations with myself.

I would say, "Tomaz, you shouldn't spend more for a good ukulele than a bad breakfast."

Things like that, things I thought Robert Bly would like.

Of course, I didn't know Robert Bly then, even though he kept entering my dreams.

Once, maneuvering a flying motorcycle over a mountainous Frankenstein terrain.

Another time, opening and closing a car door for my wife at least a hundred times.

She was naked and liking it.

Or he'd leap from a cloud to play catch with my son.

"O Silent One, O He Who Knows Nothing," he would scowl, as I practiced "Dueling Bashōs" on my blues harmonica, or fondled the stone breasts of a snow woman he'd constructed.

Awake, I wrote about octopi, miniature conifers, the rubbery wings of a bat.

But, still, he entered my dreams, dissatisfied, chasing my wife around the backyard or measuring the shadow of a stick with my traitorous son.

I wrote a poem called "The Banshi Pig Dance," which he said lacked "sacred space between words."

I practiced walking like a penguin, but he said, "The memory of an insult hurts worse than the insult."

I didn't know what that meant, but my wife and son did, curled around him like worms feasting on an apple.

All this happening the year I began calling myself Tomaz, the year I began having lengthy public conversations with myself.

Crazy Little Thing Called Love

I trapped the word called "love" in a jar, then placed it in a museum where patrons set off alarms by coming too close.

I gave a speech about the Five Kinds of Love but couldn't remember the fifth.

So I broke the jar and donned my ragged Stetson, drifting toward a picture window lit by two glasses of red wine.

And is that my wife in her red satin nightie?

And oh, Sweet Thing, did I spell nightie right?

Which makes her laugh.

Tonight, nothing hateful to stain our canvas of love— just a little bad-girl poetry with optional ice.

Good Old Days

If I ever think of the "good old days," of conversations that shook me to the bone or made me run home to make love to my wife, those conversations won't be with poets, that's for sure.

With priests either (except for one).

No, there'll be no poets or priests in my pantheon.

Just a bunch of nobodies who made me laugh, like this old guy repeating, "Shit, dammit," amazed as my son reels in another fish.

There'll be no philosophers either, except for my dead friend Neil who said starfish can have as many as fifty arms.

We were at the beach, waiting for a metaphor to wash up on shore, or a stranded seal we might resuscitate.

"Sometimes," Neil said, "you spend years tracing the roots of a tree only to find out it's a tree."

"Most definitely," I replied, "like when I had my aura photographed in Las Vegas. It looked and vibrated like a jellyfish, yet I knew it was just an aura."

He nodded, and we laughed, haply hip to the moment.

The kind of laughter I'll never share with a poet or priest.

The kind that branches out and trembles, lasting for weeks.

The Search for the Truth Continues

I believe in the life of the soul.

I even believe in God.

Thor, too, and I tremble every time his hammer thunders.

I also believe Jesus is everywhere.

This Christ is snatching cigarette butts from the sidewalk.

This other Jesus wears red stilettos—her teeth, sharper than her tongue.

And then there's Atheist Jesus, who believes having no answer is the answer.

He's the Jesus who wrote the "I Hate All Towelheads Polka," the "Kill All Faggots Hop."

He works the counter at Cumberland Farms and has a toupee that looks like a tarantula.

So many Jesuses, it's best to retire to my little cottage in Whatville where maple leaves hum a music only I can hear, and Japanese zelkovas are just a stroll away.

Where strawberries flourish in boot-sucking mud, and ants are preparing a pilgrimage—tiny white crosses on their backs.

Museum of Hard Knocks

for Charles Simic

In a museum far away people stare at a slab of lard encased in a plastic container, trying to make sense of it.

A man in a faux-python tank top contemplates a blue neon sign with "Handsome Hansom" scrawled across it.

He's sick of beating his wife, angry they arrested his pet alligator for chewing on a neighborhood toddler.

The woman he's come to meet is howling under an enormous tinfoil moon.

She's crazy, but prettier than any planet you can imagine.

The New Curator stands quietly in the middle of the room.

The Old Curator's impaled on a pitchfork positioned upside down in a pile of leaves.

When you push a button a child's voice croons, "It's easy to die when you know you're going to rise from the dead."

In this garden, there is no serpent to blame.

Just a bald, tuxedoed museum guard manning the exit door, barking out, as he boots people into the night: "And now for some real pain."

Field Trip

"It's sure cold," the cemetery guard says, "but at least it's not snowing."

A comment suggesting our lives are better than we think, when often they aren't.

Instead, the wind howling through pin oaks and sugar gum trees that wear name tags and sway and stagger like drunken conventioneers.

I point out a monument to my son, omitting that a year ago a woman was raped and beaten to death as these same trees looked on.

It was hot that night, the gates locked, which accounted for people saying, *What was she doing there, anyway?*

Today is a field trip of sorts.

Our microscope needs feeding: a dead leaf or pine cone, maybe a disembodied claw.

I like to think she had a fight with her boyfriend, then disappeared over a wall of rocks, wanting to shake him up.

It was just a "stupid thing," I want to tell my son, thinking there should be a special word for such a "stupid thing."

A word that would resonate through time, like the cry of a child falling from a thirty-story window.

Bad Behavior

When will the cops, asleep or gliding down asphalt pavements, get the call?

A little thing, an episode: many drinks, a few pills, a bit of playful grappling.

Later they made love when she was half-asleep, or maybe unconscious.

He's not sure.

This confession over a mean cup of java in an understated coffee house when we could be watching an up-and-coming minor leaguer punish a fastball.

"She's my ex-wife," he says. "We'll laugh about this later. She may not even remember."

He let himself go when he moved out, abandoning his Bowflex and West Coast diet books.

No more barbecues in the backyard where we'd get drunk and watch our grandchildren lunge at each other with Styrofoam swords.

No more roasting marshmallows over a jerry-built brazier.

I want to tell him I'm not the concierge, nor do I have the key to the secret garden, and I'm still waiting for the *Grammar of Marriage* book to arrive.

And every time I see her, I'll look away, or stare into my PalmPilot, which is really my palm, hoping for directions on how to behave.

Or how not to.

The New York School Poem

I had a favorite poet until he kept writing about his friends, Beau and Binkie.

About how they got drunk and tweezered hair from their noses, then thought they'd discovered a new way to make love, not realizing the Neanderthals had invented it.

Yeah, I liked this poet until he described how Gloria got knocked up by Chrétien, who mainlined heroin into his temple while "Walk on the Wild Side" blared in the background.

And how Chrétien survived, so Rashid wrote a song about it, which he'd chant at the end of Chrétien's readings.

Boy, I would have liked this poet more if he hadn't felt obliged to write about Mahi's depression memorabilia, which he stole from scenes of real suicides.

Or about how Joanie, after a near-death experience, believed the best part of her had come back as a car alarm.

Or if he'd just been happy to be another Bukowski—a drunk who didn't care if anyone read his poems, and who despised his friends and ex-girlfriends even more than his friends and ex-girlfriends despised him.

The Worst Love Poem Ever Written

I come to you like a coyote with one leg, wound tighter than Lady Gaga's thong, while in the sky a hot-air balloon hisses *The language of love is the language of love.*

And if I say, "Meet me at the golf simulator on Deck 13," don't affect ignorance, though love is like that, as I, like a rubber-soled elephant trainer, weep to see the dinghy of your love disappear.

Where?

Behind that cloud, that wave.

An argument would help, or a blind date with oneself. *Dave, stop. Stop, will you? Will you stop, Dave? I'm afraid.*

That movie was great and always makes me think of you, which raises the question: "Who sunk the male boat?"

Yes, I said that, in spite of the condom stuck to the floor like a deflated raft.

In spite of our labial exercises, mostly arriving during sleep, like a posse of reporters awaiting a drive-by beheading.

Bestir! my love-brain cools in the wine cellar of your tornadic frown.

I'm talking about Valentine's Day when you gave me morning glories that overtook the house.

You said you had a craving for glassware, for ebony canes, and flat screen TVs, while the frigid lovebirds sang all day in falsetto.

In return, I gave you the square root of possibility and a noun which could save the world if only I knew how to pronounce it.

A word that would replace the one called Love.

Love: an old man with a broken wrist, his white beard glimmering in the moonlight.

Oh, yeah.

PART II

The Aim

The aim is always heartless, like desire.

This morning the President is tweeting, looking for trouble.

You want to say, "Not again." "This has to stop." "Fuck off, I'm so very tired of you."

But it's 3 a.m., and there's the possibility your son's heart may stop at any moment.

There's also the dog, who's snoring under your feet and will be dead by Thanksgiving.

Whereupon Sorrow, like the heavy granite slab you'll place over her grave.

Nothing to do but pet her, promise to meet on the Rainbow Bridge, to bring your token and photos from your whole wondrous life.

Anything to distract you from that shadow prowling by the woodshed.

An itinerant angel?

An artist starving for attention, pacing the dark recesses of his cruel cage?

No, just a gaunt coyote squatting near a graveyard—stiffening at the sounds the dead make.

A Nun to Be Named Later

I've been thinking about the nun who wouldn't let me pee in fifth grade.

There is no need to know her name.

She is dead and most of her clumsy cruelties have died with her.

But tell me: Who can you trust?

I trust the geese who are too stupid to migrate this winter.

I double-park to say hello.

I want to explain that I'm on a quest for authenticity.

They're stumbling about, cold but apparently very happy.

They are like the lilies of the field, and so on and so forth.

I go back to the car and listen to a Miles Davis CD.

Supposedly, Miles stopped playing when he could no longer hear the music.

Was he telling the truth?

The truth is her name was Sister Josepha.

It makes no sense to hold a grudge.

Breakfast with Dad

Yesterday the sky was as gray and seamless as a poorly done facelift.

It was late afternoon and I was rattling the cages of child-friendly things to do.

I was thinking of those luxurious spots at the edge of glaciers where not much happens.

That's how to stay young, my *Old Guy's Manual for Staying Young* says.

Pain in the groin, pain in the L-3 vertebra, spots on my face like puke-brown barnacles on a seaside rock.

You know the indignities.

Or will shortly.

Face it, the old earth-shattering ideas have left town or can't find a place to crash-land.

They hover like cigarette smoke above a hysterical cocktail party as a self-absorbed soccer mom lies about giving birth to twins on a grass tennis court.

Well, my dear, I have my stories, too.

This one happened at the Breakfast Nook where an exquisite one-armed waitress was serving us.

My father gave her a hundred-dollar bill for two eight-dollar omelets and said, "What's mine is yours."

She smiled and brought back the change. "He always does this," she said.

This event, which happened many years ago, is just an afterthought now, though still demanding to be translated.

31

Isn't that what we're supposed to do? Try to find meaning with our eyelids half closed?

I will tell you: There is more meaning in an empty birdfeeder than in those small-print fat books, heavy with ideas.

I turned to them often during my father's last days, searching for the courage to let him go.

Before Anyone Had Ever Heard of Johnny Depp

I'm trying to find a runway that's not in flux, some place I can strut my stuff.

Like that roofless bar in Hermosa Beach.

It was called La Paz or La Place, or maybe *Je Vous Demande Pardon* since I'm always seeking forgiveness.

Whatever, it had the best taco burritos in southern California and was manned by a bartender with a pop-star face and a vicious overhead volleyball serve.

I was explaining this to a classmate at my 48th high-school reunion.

His name was Mario, a guy as fidgety as a conductor's wand, intent on settling his nerves with a tumbler of gin and tonic.

He called me a liar, and that's when we attracted a crowd of old guys who still believed in signs and symbols.

Undeterred, I recounted my idyllic nights at the *Je Vous Demande Pardon* until they told me to shut up unless I had something lyrical to say.

Exhaling deeply, I let it rip:

"It was the Summer of Relief when Uncle Lou came stumbling out of the closet wearing two different shoes and the sun bore down on us like some mythological god. 'O Hope! O, Charity,' the birdies sang…," and I could've gone on if not interrupted by smatterings of laughter and a wall of gray suits drifting toward a table of Buffalo chicken wings.

I felt hurt until I realized we'd all be dead in ten years or found heavily sedated, wandering around parking garages unable to locate our cars.

We'd all like to be as permanent as a forehead crease, as necessary as a mop in a house that's sprung a leak.

Who wants to end up as an unsung artificial leg dragged across some stranger's straw rug?

Forty-eight years ago, back in Hermosa Beach, I was drunk on tequila with a wino named Sudsy.

We were stealing two-by-fours from a construction site.

We were piling them like blocks of letters that once correctly organized might form a word to explain our sorry-ass lives.

All this before the age of flat stomachs and unpronounceable coffee drinks.

The age my *Old Guy Manual on Memory* lovingly refers to as "Pre-Lacunal."

Words of Wisdom from the Lost Land between Your Ears

My father once said, "I alone beweep my outcast state."

Okay, he never said that but at least it's a place to start.

Better than those lyrical hip thrusts that, in my humble opinion, weigh down a poem like huge blocks of flesh the unimaginative call whales.

I had a friend who wrote a whole book of poems about whales.

Then he killed himself.

Which is also a lie.

But here's something that's true.

Last night I read about a Lakota teenager who's more than happy to freeze her ass off in a tiny canvas tent to protect us from extinction.

Makes me want to get on a plane and fly west, open my '60s war chest and reclaim my mukluks and cowboy hat I bought on opening day of Disney World.

Which was on October 1, 1971, if you're interested.

It's funny how you can fashion yourself a hero of the proletariat or a philosopher king for only so long. Then age sets in and you become as slow-witted and boring as a Neanderthal staring endlessly into his sacred fire.

I'd like to tell this girl that you don't have to be standing next to a horse to hear its weeping.

I want to take a deep breath and say, "I don't know what's holding us up, but I trust it will stand firm."

Which is of course claptrap.

Because we know the pipes will be shipped, and the crude oil will flow under rivers like a black alien virus.

We know it can't be stopped, any more than these Lakota teenagers—their campfire faces stubborn as stars that dutifully watch over us no matter how stupid we are.

The Rapture

Cereal aisles confuse me, as do people who say they've returned from the dead for "one more try."

That's what this guy is saying as he leans against a porcelain sink, divining meaning from the mist rising from my urinal.

He has two plastic eyes sewn onto a face that glows like a new basketball, and I'm waiting for him to punch me in the back of the head.

I'm at the airport, trying to remember where I'm supposed to be.

That all-too-common confusion, like when you discover the owner of Billy's Grill is named Angelo.

And now this guy.

He's waiting for a trumpet to sound. Until then, he's followed me into my favorite restaurant.

It's a place called Angelo's owned by a guy named Billy.

He says, "All the nations on earth are in mourning."

"I can accept that," I say, feigning interest while licking a last spoonful of clam chowder.

Trust me, my friends, I, too, am aware of that encroaching white light this guy says we come from.

How, like a hooker, it never stops whispering into my bad ear.

I, too, am aware of Mr. Death hovering over my bed at three in morning, bragging about the size of his penis as my old-fashioned mahogany clock cracks its knuckles.

There used to be a ringing in my ears. Now a hoarse

laughter like post-nuclear waves crashing on shore.

Annoyed, I ask him to pass the salt but he says it's "out of reach"—no doubt code words for the Great Beyond.

Or at least that's what my *Old Guy's Manual to Life after Death* says, though with so many people being resurrected it's hard to believe anything anymore.

The One That Got Away

I was sixteen and had a crush on a Ukrainian girl.

She's probably dead by now or fat, though maybe she's slim and classy and owns a Pilates studio.

Sometimes when I'm stressing a bicep at the goddam YMCA with its poor ventilation system and teenage goons, I expect to look up and see her winking at me as she punishes the hip adductor machine with deep scissor-like thrusts.

That's how we carried on during those midnight rendezvous in a soot-covered city made famous after some poor bastard missed a field goal wide right.

If I saw her tomorrow sashaying in a pair of heart-thumping red yoga pants down the Boulevard of Old Guy Memories, I'd kneel and take her hand.

I'd kiss the pinkie I so often suckled, thinking I was being homeopathic or part of some great revolution that, like all revolutions, service only men.

"My apologies, Mademoiselle," I'd say stupidly, pretending that the black hole between us wasn't as vast as the distance between who I am and who I wanted to be.

The Abductee

Grandmothers line the street squawking like blue jays.

They're fed up, and who can blame them, with so many dogs wandering the countryside, unwanted.

Their husbands slouch in rusty wheelchairs facing the gray concrete walls of our sick-weary hospitals.

They're staring at what? What?

Yet we keep their organs alive until they wrinkle and collapse like three-day-old balloons.

We construct birdfeeders outside their windows, believing they can distinguish between an oriole and a squirrel.

There was a man.

A friend of a friend's friend who happened to end up at my house.

He looked like my sister's old bulldog, who itself looks like a convict.

Still, I had to reach out after he confessed to being an alien abductee.

It's the kind of thing you envy.

We circled the Weber Grill like two codependent planets crisscrossing a galaxy whose death was as certain and unplanned as a mugshot.

The conversation got heavy as I kebabbed and curried a fistful of rucola and dandelions, a potion my *Old Guy Book on Longevity* says counters the ravages of estrogen.

But it was hard to concentrate with all his talk about mind scans and hybrid sex.

Especially since I'd had such high hopes for the evening.

And what an evening it was, the stars blinking their strange Morse code as we leaned drunkenly against each other waiting for something interstellar to happen.

Wordmeister

He dusts the shelves where his books used to be.

He had some big ones—rock-hard abs, too—and he could half-nelson a cliché until it screamed "mama."

He was the Word's most wanted man.

Could steam into a library and shake up the joint.

A rose broke into spasm when he read a poem about a rose breaking into spasm.

There was a beautiful blonde in the front row, with earrings fashioned from tiny No. 2 pencils.

She had lapis-lazuli eyes, her fingers bleeding from a thorn on a red rose she was womanhandling.

He read a poem about wanting to be a woman in love with other women.

He believed the phrase "flattened by a sacrament" could distract a terrorist.

That the right word could bring the whole world down (or together).

That he could let the stale air out of a century by just giving it a name.

All of this long before he had his teeth whitened and was given the Blowhard Emeritus Chair at the local college.

Now just these empty bookshelves, a duster dangling limply from his hand, and the image of a red rose quivering like a plucked guitar string in the hands of a beautiful and troubled woman.

Anniversary

What did she think about when she stumbled alone into the woods?

Her red dress?

His hard blue suit tangoing on a parquet floor?

The handsome art historian she'd left behind?

Or did she consider the endless parade of diapers and jammed toddler car seats?

Or her husband's mindless groping in the darkest hours of the night?

Perhaps all she wanted was the possibility of a simple cup of chai in an empty house.

He told the police they had argued about McDonald's after loading up the van.

It was their anniversary, and they'd been camping with their four young children.

He said they were a happy couple and rarely fought, but McDonald's was not "acceptable," and she should've known that.

She should've been happy to make chicken salad sandwiches with Wonder Bread, but instead she inexplicably and quietly entered the woods.

He couldn't leave the children to follow her, could he?

Three days later they found her in an airport hotel, clenching a one-way ticket to Las Vegas.

She'd had her nails done, and the room was strewn with Happy Meal boxes and half-eaten, room-service entrees.

She swore she'd go home, eventually.

She had even saved the McToys for her children, whom she loved and missed terribly.

But they couldn't *make* her go home, could they?

Certainly she hadn't broken any laws.

Remembrance of Things Past for an Audience of One

"Bridge Over Troubled Water."

Man, that song hit me like a flatiron thrown by a hippie-girl in a floral print muumuu with a giant daisy in her hair and a bad case of the clap.

The Sixties!

I know what you're thinking: another old guy with the doughnut appetite of a cop and an inclination toward hyperbole.

A guy who can't quite grasp that long hair on a sixty-six-year-old man makes him look like one of The Three Stooges.

"And lose those sideburns," some punk tells me in front of the local convenience store.

It started innocently enough with him not holding the door for me and saying something about being blinded by the glare from my bald spot.

I called him a thug, and he said I looked like Friar Tuck, so he was at least well-read.

What else could he do?

Beat up an old man?

Instead, he joined a group of itchy-fingered boys who were oblivious to the scuffle about to take place.

The girls were worse, leaning against a red Range Rover bragging about their hairless legs and lip gloss.

It was a knucklehead moment.

All of us frozen in time like a bunch of skinned chickens hanging by their ankles.

Someone had to be the adult, so I said, "If there were still such things as winding sheets, our skin would gladly embrace them, so relax, dude. We're all in this together."

The last I saw of them they were admiring their cell phones, stumbling like blind salmon up a newly paved road.

Call Me

Gutters buried under snow, foot-long icicles falling to the ground like misdirected ICBMs.

And where was I the day the world went cold and brittle?

Call me Anonymous, call me Lack of Self-Control, but don't call me late for The Final Showdown, which I insist is right around the corner.

But listen …

Once, I was a magician at rich kids' parties—had a rabbit, a top hat, a series of silly jokes, yet always kicked out before the cake was cut.

I was a one-man ad for Poetry's Last Tour, wore black, pointed Italian shoes my son sent from Venice, investigated Robert Frost sightings, examining every stone wall, every leaf and sapling.

Now I lie in bed, slurping cough medicine and watching "This Dumb Old House" reruns while throwing darts at spiders just for the fun of it.

I'm waiting for The Question, The Answer.

A black file folder with my name on it, a sad-sack story with no beginning or end …

Friends

I like my friends best when they're depressed.

They're easy to be with when the gun's cocked, loaded, and sleeping under their pillows.

When something as trivial as an impacted wisdom tooth makes them ponder the Great Beyond where most Americans believe there's a 77% chance of meeting God.

"It's the 23% that keeps us going," I tell them, as we sip weak tea, pretending to be children with a great capacity for love, hoping our hearts might explode from our chests and soar like fist-sized red balloons.

I like my friends best when they're trembling.

When their sense of self-worth hangs by the thread of a thread.

When the mention of a broken baby monitor hooked up to an empty room can bring them to tears.

When they're at their lowest, that's when I like my friends.

That's when I know they'll need me.

Bedtime Story

Choose a "cheery daydream," your manual suggests, like cannonballing into a vat of peanut butter or soaking your toes in a pool of strawberry Jell-O while your dog laps rainwater off the driveway.

Take deep breaths, Dr. Swami says.

Give your Chakra a name, something cute like "Star-Filled" or "Heaven-Sent."

Your checkbook is fat and the fridge is overflowing.

So don't fret when airplanes crash into buildings and restaurants ignite in places like Basrah and Mosul.

Just pretend the maple trees are singing nursery rhymes in French.

Or make a simple snack of coleslaw on a whole wheat bun while shouting, "I spot a righteous metaphor off to starboard," hoping you can think of one, as you stretch out among night crawlers and daddy-long-legs—darkness approaching with its sharp black claws …

Last Will and Testament

To my first divorce lawyer, a pair of cement shoes.

To my accountant, fess up to hitting on my ex-wife.

And to you, my son, of course we knew the smell of cannabis and why the cellar window was ajar.

Make way for stupid!

Which is better than being called a loser—my nickname senior year after delivering a Freudian interpretation of Led Zeppelin's "A Whole Lotta Love," which got me brass-knuckled out of my class presidency—the next morning, waking to a chorus of blue jays screeching, "No, No, No," my head about to pop like a piñata.

And to Father Torquemada, "Yes, I have sinned, indiscriminately."

And to Coach Dipshit, "Losing's making a comeback."

Yet here I am, forty-eight years later, still searching for the nerve center to the Wonka factory, gazing through a rusty telescope at the Eternal Nothing, just one baby step ahead of the maggots …

The Heebie-Jeebies

It's early morning when it arrives.

Uninvited, as usual.

So why so surprised?

Why up so fast like a tripped mousetrap?

And what's that thunder between his ears that others call thought?

I remember the first time, like finding myself in a huge walk-in clinic where everyone was wearing black leather masks.

I was never the same again, though I won't tell him that.

Better to pass on the optimism of a young Buddha than this crummy gene.

No reason to hold out one's arms and pretend to be a crucifix or act like you're stuck in an all-night bar with your legs chained to a barstool.

When I was his age my mother said, "Speak to God. He's always listening."

But I left that heavy lifting to her.

Because sometimes you need someone to yank up the rope ladder behind you.

That's what I tell him as I read aloud from the third chapter of *My Old-Guy Guide to Falling Apart,* appropriately called "How to Ward off Anxiety."

Mostly useless advice, yet it gives us something to do while killing what's left of darkness, hoping we might stumble upon the right spell.

The Hero with One or Two Faces

I like those mornings when it's just me and the dog.

When I'm shoveling Froot Loops into the pie-hole of a face I call "Me."

When for a few minutes I don't feel wrongly made or have to wonder why that dimple girls found so cute is now situated in the general vicinity of my double chin.

I'm at the grocery store with my wife.

They're out of Froot Loops, but there's this guy who says he's found a secret stash.

"It's somewhere by the prunes," he says.

His head is shaped like a lightbulb, and his face is so wrinkled it looks like a fingerprint.

Still, he fashions himself charming as he eye-gropes my wife's ass.

I should be mad, but all I can think of is last night, the moon so pregnant I thought it might burst.

The kind of experience that makes you want to shapeshift into one of those undifferentiatedly happy creatures found only in cartoons.

To be anywhere but with a wife who's clearly annoyed by my penchant for blowing things up.

She's wearing a white halter top, a silk number that a French anthropologist might describe as "autochthonous," though this oaf is too dumb to make that leap.

The next time I see him is in the checkout line.

He's holding a box of Froot Loops, which I wrestle from him before getting into some serious hand-to-hand, as my wife heads for the exit—the customers and cashiers frozen like creatures on the walls of the Lascaux caves.

Sisyphus

The idea was to write an Old School New School Poem, none of that fashionable irony where poets sit around their endowed swimming pools laughing at the rest of us who have kids and work for a living.

Who don't have the money or time or the inclination to meet a terribly confused coed at the local No-Tell Motel.

Who have a real pet instead of some stupid cat named Shakespeare.

Hey, I'm just being honest.

But back to the Old School New School Poem.

On second thought, I already wrote that poem.

Let's talk about Sisyphus.

Camus said the myth of Sisyphus proves there's "no fate that cannot be surmounted by scorn."

He said Sisyphus reached a place of contented acceptance.

He said, "One must imagine Sisyphus happy."

But what about the fucking boulder?

What about the unheavenly heaviness in Sisyphus's legs and arms?

What about that archetypal sweat stinging his eyes?

Or the stars looking down on him, hugging themselves against that bowel-loosening chill pale-faced, anorexic philosophers call angst?

What kind of idiot would argue that Sisyphus "surmounted" anything, much less scorn?

Certainly, Sisyphus would've gladly passed off the boulder to Camus, or pissed on his many books of false prophecies.

That would've been a very different story, don't you think?

One brimming with the kind of heroism even I'd have to admire.

Moments Recollected in Hostility

I once had a custom-made bumper sticker that read, "Good Luck with the New Cat."

It was meant to enlighten people as they flitted down the highway, panting like terrified kites caught in a vicious, indifferent breeze.

My purpose, as always, was to plant a necessary metaphor in a bamboo field of possibilities in an attempt to force even one or two dimwits to hack away at it.

How much better it would be if you could say, "The hole in the knee of the jeans was merely purchased," and a few adventurous souls would wrestle with the grounds of likeness, instead of engaging in an episode of road rage ending with a troubled motorist reaching for his crossbow.

How much better to convince someone that the meaning of life can be found in, "Swing hard and always remember to draw the curtains."

This is what we get instead: "Today the President's advisers said the bombing sends a clear message 'There's a new sheriff in town.'"

Who talks like that anymore except the kind of sadist who would get a cheap laugh by holding up a mirror to the terrified mug of a puppy?

And yet ... behold my beloved working-class, as they march in lockstep over a cliff while their leader drifts harmlessly to safety in his golden parachute.

While his minions tighten their exquisite silk ties on their way to an amphitheater where they'll argue like little boys over who can hold their pee the longest.

Which brings me back to my bumper sticker and how happy I was on that beautiful April day driving through hill and dale repeating, "Good luck with the new cat, Good luck with the new cat," as if the future of the world depended on deciphering its meaning.

Domestic

We've joined hands around a warped Ouija board, inquiring where the phrase "for crying out loud" comes from.

We're always saying it to each other, always mad about something, except at breakfast when we eat our complex carbohydrates while constructing pyramids of excuses and regrets.

Sometimes something offensive escapes our teenager's lips, but mostly he's happy, eating Cheerios, smiling at the dog.

Moments like these I embrace the seamless blend of nonsense we call life, or recount the good old days when I delivered seventy-five newspapers by 7 a.m., then did 110 pushups with a 50-pound bag of sand on my back.

That's the kind of guy my teenager would respect.

The over-the-hill stud my wife will crawl under the sheets with, the rose-colored sheets I've fashioned into a tent, under which her spine softens, her calves relax, while I tell her everything she wants to hear.

Coda

Happy

Gentle Reader,

In spite of persistent rumors, let me assure you that I am happy.

Happy as the Brazilian beauty in a red thong cavorting half-naked on the Travel Channel.

Happy as the local loony screaming at the same tree every morning, convinced it's an enemy from a past life.

I'm happy I can say, "Don't go away I've got the baddest poem right here in my back pocket," and no one thinks I'm nuts.

Happy for artificial putting greens, yellow buses that swallow up children yet no one gets hurt.

Happy for tuna fish and the piano player at Nordstrom who asked me to sing along.

Crusty sand dunes, orchids, a solitary grayish cloud frozen in the sky—I'm happy for them.

Happy for the rust-colored bottom of a rap diva, for the ant-sized beauty mark on my wife's bum.

Happy a sixty-six-year-old man can dance and play air guitar in his boxer shorts while his teenage son laughs himself silly.

Even happy for Plan A, though I'll never understand it, and for the chance—no, pleasure—to spend a few idle moments inside this here ellipsis …

Acknowledgments

Some of the previous prose poems or versions of those prose poems have previously appeared in:

5 a.m.: "My Father Wasn't an Alcholic."

TriQuarterly: "And Nothing Else Matters," "Neil," and "Happy."

Witness: "Cheerleader."

Mississippi Review: "The Robert Bly Affair."

Another Chicago Magazine: "Wordmeister."

Green Mountains Review: "Hurricane" and "Call Me."

Mudlark: "Heraclitus," "Breakfast with Dad," "The One That Got Away," "The Abductee," "Remembrance of Things Past for an Audience of One," and "Before Anyone Had Ever Heard of Johnny Depp."

Alembic: "Houdini Weenie" and "American Male, Acting Up."

DMQ: "Love Story" and "Domestic."

Caesura: "Last Will and Testament."

One (More) Glass (a broadside on glass): "Bedtime Story."

Web Del Sol: "Talkin' 'Bout My Generation."

trampset: "The Heebie-Jeebies,"

Many of the poems in Part I, or versions of them, appeared in the "New" section of *Rants and Raves: Selected and New Prose Poems by Peter Johnson* (White Pine Press, 2010).

"American Male, Acting Up" was also published as a broadside designed by Stephen Frech.

About the Author

Peter Johnson has published four books of prose poems, five novels, a book of short stories, and two chapbooks. His second book of prose poems, *Miracles & Mortifications,* received the James Laughlin Award from The Academy of American Poets, and he was founder and editor of *The Prose Poem: An International Journal.* Past issues can be found at https://digitalcommons. providence.edu/prosepoem/. His work has received creative writing fellowships from the National Endowment for the Arts and the Rhode Island Council on the Arts, along with a "Best Book of 2012" citation by *Kirkus Reviews.* News about his poetry and fiction can be found at peterjohnsonauthor.com